Roads

Nicola Baxter

FRANKLIN WATTS

LONDON • SYDNEY

This edition 2003

Franklin Watts
96 Leonard Street
London
EC2A 4XD

Franklin Watts Australia
45-51 Huntley Street
Alexandria
NSW 2015

Copyright © Franklin Watts 2000

ISBN 0 7496 4996 8

A CIP catalogue for this book is
available from the British Library

Printed in Hong Kong, China

Series editor: Anderley Moore
Assistant editor: Enid Fisher
Series designer: John Christopher, WHITE DESIGN
Picture research: Sue Mennell

Picture Credits

Cover: Arcaid/Richard Bryant/Courtesy of Schindler's Lifts
(main image), Still Pictures/John Isaac (inset)

Interior Pictures:
Illustrations: Peter Bull: 6-7 (timeline), 8, 10, 11, 24, 25.
Sarah John: 7, 9, 12, 14, 22.
Photography: AKG Photo, London 8 (Eric Lessing);
Associated Press 19 (The Charlotte Observer); Ecoscene;
4t (Andrew D.R. Brown), 11 (Chinch Gryniewicz), 18
(Nick Hawkes); Mary Evans Picture Library 9b (Hilary
Evans); Ronald Grant Archive 7 (Courtesy Time
Warner/Wizard of Oz); Robert Harding Picture Library
29t; David Noble 20, 26; Panos Pictures 9t (Caroline
Penn); Scottish Highland Photo Library 23; Skyscan
Photolibrary 4b (APS, UK), 13t (Ian Yates), 13b; Still
Pictures 6 (John Isaac), 12 (Romani Cagnoni), 27 (Mark
Edwards), 28l (Nick Cobbing), 28r, 29b.

Contents

On the road 4–5

Road routes 5

From near and far 6–7

Roads of adventure 7

Roads old and new 8–13

Roman roads 8
The age of road building 10
Roads for Motor Vehicles 11
Road planning 13

Road signs 14–15

What do they mean? 14

Road maps 16–17

Danger on the roads 18–19

Roads all around us 26–27

What's more... 28–29

Glossary 30–31

Index 32

Road names 20–21

The road of life 22–23

Road robbers 24–25

Highwaymen 24
The tale of black Bart 25

On the road

From the earliest times, people have felt the need to travel. They made tracks across the countryside and gradually, as towns and cities sprang up, these tracks became roads, used by carts and carriages as well as people on foot. Today, bicycles, cars, buses and trucks speed along our roads, which need to be strong, smooth and safe.

◆ New roads are built with heavy traffic in mind. They help to keep vehicles on the move by avoiding sharp bends, steep hills and hold-ups at junctions.

◆ Many of today's roads were once dirt trails used by people and animals. They are often narrow and winding, skirting obstacles such as rocks, water, trees and hills.

Road words

Many different words are used to describe roads and their uses in this book. Can you find the ones below on the following pages and discover what they mean?

Camber	Juggernaut
Pilgrimage	Network
Tarmac	Crosswind
Junction	Slip road
Trading	Bitumen
Route	Highwayman

Road routes

Look at this map showing the main roads of an area. Can you answer the questions below? (Answers on page 30.)

Reading the Road

1 *Why do so many roads cross the centre of the area?*

2 *Do travellers from north to south of the area have to go through the main city?*

3 *Why do you think several roads run to the coast?*

Try This!

Look at a map of the area where you live. What does the pattern of roads tell you?

YOU CAN TRY THIS!

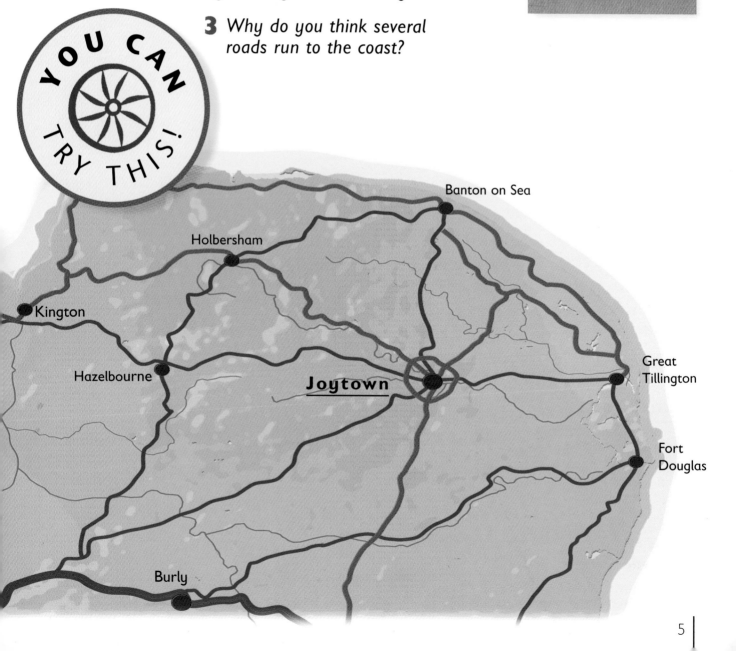

Banton on Sea

Holbersham

Kington

Hazelbourne

Joytown

Great Tillington

Fort Douglas

Burly

From near and far

Just as people have developed easier and faster means of travel for themselves, they have also invented new ways to transport goods. These now travel quickly by air, land and sea. But only two hundred years ago, nothing could move faster than a galloping horse.

The Silk Road

From around 300 BC, merchants from Asia who wanted to trade in Europe had to transport their rare silks and spices many kilometres over mountains and deserts. This trail became known as the Silk Road.

↥ Parts of the Silk Road crossed vast areas of desert, so merchants had to use camels instead of horses or mules to transport their goods.

Road travel through the ages

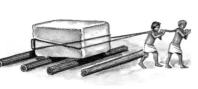

stone-age rollers

chariot

medieval wagon

stagecoach

Roads of adventure

Travelling is exciting. You never know what you might see and learn on the way. Travellers tell stories of adventures — both real and imaginary — that have happened on the road.

▶ *In the film* The Wizard of Oz, *Dorothy's journey along the Yellow Brick Road leads to adventures and meetings with amazing characters.*

Try This!

Write a poem or draw a picture to show what excites you about being on the road — even on the shortest journey.

The Golden Journey to Samarkand

The travellers describing their journey in this extract from the poem *The Road to Samarkand*, are excited by the idea of finding new things.

Sweet to ride forth at evening from the wells
When shadows pass gigantic on the sand,
And softly through the silence beat the bells
Along the Golden Road to Samarkand.

We travel not for trafficking [trading] alone:
By hotter winds our fiery hearts are fanned:
For lust of knowing what should not be known
We make the Golden Journey to Samarkand.

JAMES ELROY FLECKER

penny farthing bicycle   Ford Model T   motor bus   four-wheel drive

Roads old and new

Roman roads

Between about 275 BC and AD 200, the Roman Empire spread over much of Europe and parts of Asia and Africa.

To control such a large area, an army had to travel quickly over great distances, so the Romans built the biggest network of roads the world had ever seen. They were straight, going over hills in places, instead of through valleys. This made it harder for enemies to surprise the marching army and reduced the time it took to get from place to place.

➥ *How the Romans made their roads.*

Curved surface so rainwater runs off into ditches.

Paving stones set in mortar to make road surface smooth.

➤ *Many Roman roads still survive. This one in Greece shows its original stone surface. Others are still in use today, but have been resurfaced to cope with modern traffic.*

Layer of flat stones.

Crushed stone and rubble rammed into a firm layer.

Number work

If the Roman army could march at 7 km an hour for 8 hours a day, how many days would it take to complete these journeys?

• **London to York 308 km**

• **Paris to Marseille 784 km**

• **Rome to Athens 2,352 km**

Journeys with a meaning

By the Middle Ages, most roads were much worse than in Roman times – little more than muddy tracks. Journeys that take only hours today could take days. Longer journeys could take weeks.

▲ *In parts of Egypt, pilgrims paint their houses with scenes of their journey to the holy city of Mecca.*

Try This!

Why not design your own badge showing a place you have been to by road? Choose a symbol or scene that really sums up a place, such as a building or a flag.

YOU WILL NEED:

- card
- pens, paints or crayons
- a safety pin
- sticky tape
- scissors

Cut out your badge shape from the card and colour in your picture. Fix the safety pin to the other side with some sticky tape.

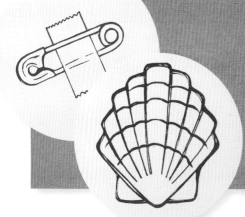

Pilgrimages – journeys to religious shrines – were popular in medieval times. Muslims hoped to visit Mecca; Christians would travel to Canterbury in England and Santiago de Compostela in Spain; Jerusalem was special to both Muslims and Christians, and to Jewish people. Travel was on foot or, for the wealthy few, in rough carts. Either way, it was uncomfortable.

◀ *The cockle-shell badge on this pilgrim's hat shows he has visited the Shrine at Santiago de Compostela.*

The age of roadbuilding

Roadbuilding began to improve in the eighteenth century. The beginning of the Industrial Revolution meant that more people and goods were on the move, usually in horse-drawn wagons. Mass-produced items such as pottery needed better roads if they were to reach their customers in one piece!

By the 19th century, many road surfaces were made from a layer of tar with stones in it called tarmacadam (or tarmac).

Roadbuilders preferred to create bends around hills to avoid steep climbs that would be difficult for horses pulling carriages and carts.

The base was made of crushed stone and sand, often bound together with cement or a tar-like substance called bitumen.

The surface of the road was curved to allow water to run off and lessen the chance of flooding. This was called the camber.

Did you know...

Tarmacadam was named after the Scottish inventor John McAdam (1756–1836). He published his ideas on road surfaces in 1816, when he was building roads in Bristol, England. His methods changed the way roads were built all over the

Roads for motor vehicles

In the twentieth century, the growing numbers of motor cars and lorries soon began to damage roads designed for horse-drawn vehicles. A much stronger kind of road was needed. Modern roads designed for heavy traffic often have a concrete surface laid over a base of crushed rock called aggregate. This has the advantage that, unlike tarmac, it does not expand and move in hot weather. By putting steel bars through the concrete, roadbuilders can make roads that are strong enough to take the largest juggernauts without cracking.

Sides are landscaped to blend into the countryside. They stop strong crosswinds that could make tall vehicles hard to steer.

Roads with many lanes have crash barriers in the centre of the road to stop accidents.

Slip roads join the main road at a shallow angle so vehicles can gain speed before joining fast-moving traffic.

Roads still have a camber, but drains carry surface water away quickly.

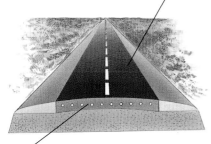

Steel bars give the road surface strength and stop the concrete shrinking as it sets.

The effects of speed

Vehicles travelling at high speed need roads that are straight and fairly flat. This can only be done in mountainous places by changing the landscape. Roadbuilders today can use huge earth-moving equipment to cut through hillsides and make tunnels through mountain ranges.

▶ *Roads that follow the natural shape of mountains are often very steep and winding.*

Try This! Feel the Force

YOU WILL NEED:

- a rectangular tray or a smooth plank of wood
- something to fit in a shoe and act as a weight, such as a stone or bag of sand
- a ruler
- a selection of boots and shoes

The force that stops things sliding over each other is called friction. Modern road surfaces have to be smooth enough for vehicles to travel quickly but give enough friction to stop them skidding. Car tyres need surfaces that will grip the road, even when it is wet.

You can find out about surfaces that prevent skidding by testing the friction between your shoes and the ground.

1 Place the shoe with a weight in it at one end of the tray or plank.

2 Slowly lift that end until the shoe begins to slip.

3 Ask a friend to measure how high the end is from the table.

4 Keep a note of your results.

The shoe with the best grip is the one you could lift highest before it began to slip. Make a graph of your results. Now try wetting the soles of the shoes and the ramp. Does it make a difference?

Road planning

Before heavy machinery was available, roadbuilding was difficult, so roads between towns and villages were built round obstacles or unsuitable ground. With the growth of cities and the large number of houses needed, improvements in roadbuilding technology have enabled planners to design road systems with a much more regular layout. This makes travel easier and quicker.

Try This!

Look at a map of your area. You may be able to find a photograph taken from an aeroplane, like those below. Can you tell if the roads are old or new?

◆ The street lights of Toronto, Canada, highlight the city-centre road pattern.

▶ Helmsley village, England, has a square where markets are held.

Spot the difference

First, look at these two pictures. One is of a city, and the other is of a village. Both photographs have been taken from an aeroplane so you can see the patterns of the roads very clearly. Compare the differences in the way that the roads have been planned.

1 *Look at the roads in the city. These areas were often planned and built over a short period of time to cater for large volumes of traffic. What do you notice about them?*

2 *Now look at the roads in the village. Can you tell which parts were built first? Why do you think the roads here look different from those in the city?*

3 *Do fast, straight roads suit all road users?*

Road signs

A

Drivers speeding down a busy road only see road signs for a few seconds, but those seconds are vital. A driver needs to understand a sign almost instantly. Pictures and colours can often give a message faster than words, especially if the driver is in a foreign country.

B

Try This!

Copy this road sign for children crossing several times on card using different bright colours.

Make one in the colours above, one with yellow people on a green background and a blue edge, and one with red people on a blue background and a black edge.

Put the signs at one end of the playground and see which is easiest to make out from far away. Remember, you could be travelling towards them at 112 km per hour. Every second counts!

Which is most important:
• the brightness of the colours?
• the contrast between the colours?

Road signs with red on them usually give a warning. In some countries, signs in the shape of a triangle also mean there may be danger ahead.

C

D

E

Try This!

Can you read the sign below quickly and easily? The lettering on road signs is just as important as any pictures. What kind of lettering is used on road signs near your school?

Look at the fonts on a computer and find some that would be suitable for road signs.

SCHOOL

F

Can you guess what these road signs from various countries mean?
(Answers on p30)

G

Road maps

Maps are very useful for planning a journey by road. They show you which direction to take to reach your destination. They also show where there are landmarks to look at on the way.

Using Scale

The scale shows how distances on the map relate to real distances on the ground. Here 1 cm = 300 metres.

```
0   300  600   900  1200 1500m
```

Using Symbols

Symbols give extra information. How many of these can you find on this map?

✝ church   ℂ telephone box
▌ railway   ✶ windmill
✈ airport   )(bridge
                  ♜ ancient monument

Try This!

Draw a map to help a visitor find your school from your home.

Newtown

High Wood

Old Forest

West Hill

Oldville

Using Colour

The colouring of areas of the map also gives information. Can you spot these?

- motorway
- main road
- minor road
- woodland or forest
- river
- lake
- built-up area
- marsh or bog

Mill Hill

North Lake

River Green

Ashton

Try This! Map Reading

1 How far is it from Newtown church to the ancient monument by road? (Use string to measure.)

2 How far is it from Oldville church to the ancient monument by road?

3 You are standing with your back to Newtown church. Turn right and travel to the junction and take the right hand turn. Take the first turning on your left, cross a bridge, then take the next right turn. What do you see?

4 You live in Ashton and want to go to North Lake for the day. If your car travels at 60 km per hour, how long will it take you to get there?

Danger on the roads

Bad road conditions or a second's lack of concentration by drivers, cyclists and motorcycle riders can cause a serious accident. When roads are packed with traffic, all these road users need to know how to react to changes safely – and fast!

Number work

Today we are used to motorists travelling at speed but have you ever considered just how fast a car might travel in one minute or even one second? Try this:

Suppose a car is travelling at 90 km an hour. Can you work out how far it will travel in just one second?

YOU CAN TRY THIS!

Try This! Design a Road Safety Poster

Road safety is very important. To learn more about this, you could take cycling proficiency lessons or ask a policeman to talk to your class about road safety.

Can you design a poster for younger children, encouraging them to be careful when crossing roads?

◄ *What has been done to make this busy road safe to cross?*

Hurricane Floyd Halts Highways

From our Weather correspondent

Two-thirds of North Carolina have been declared a disaster area following the devastation left by Hurricane Floyd, which hit the United States this week. Many rivers have burst their banks and vast areas of land are under water. One river in the Carolinas has risen to over 20 feet (7m) above flood level. Hundreds of highways across the stricken area have been closed down, and helicopters have been brought in to rescue stranded motorists.

Choppers drop emergency supplies

Flooding has made almost all country roads impassable. People marooned in townships and isolated farms are being airlifted to safety, although fears are growing for the 49 people reported missing, presumed swept away by the fast-moving floods. Residents in the worst-hit areas who cannot be reached are having food and other essential supplies dropped by fleets of choppers operating a round-the-clock emergency shuttle service.

One motorist described his ordeal:

"The speed of it was frightening. I was under water in less than a minute!"

Pender County, North Carolina

Power, telephone and water supplies have also been devastated by the severe flooding. In many areas, sewage treatment systems have been disrupted and tap water is undrinkable. Fear of disease has made the provision of fresh drinking water a priority, a government spokesman said last night.

It is likely to take months and hundreds of millions of dollars to clear the roads and repair the damage of this devastating storm.

Try This!

Try to find other news stories about events that have blocked roads. Write your own newspaper article about a dramatic event that prevents people travelling by road.

Road names

Some road names, such as North Road, London Road and Park Street, describe where the road leads.

Others have been named after a famous historical event or an important person. Can you find some of these near where you live?

Try This!

Make a list of the road names around your home or school. Can you find out where they come from? You could try:

- asking people who have lived in the area for a long time

- looking at books about the history of the area

- asking at your local library.

If a new road was built near your school, what should it be called? How would you go about finding a name that everyone would like?

Washington Square in New York is named after George Washington, the first President of the United States.

Naming by numbers

Some streets are known by numbers rather than names. In New York, for example, most roads that run from north to south are called avenues, such as Fifth Avenue. The roads running east to west are called streets, as in West 42nd Street. The distance between roads is called a block.

Number work

From the corner of Fifth Ave and East 72nd St, how many blocks is it to:

1. The corner of Madison Ave and East 57th St?

2. The corner of First Ave and East 34th St?

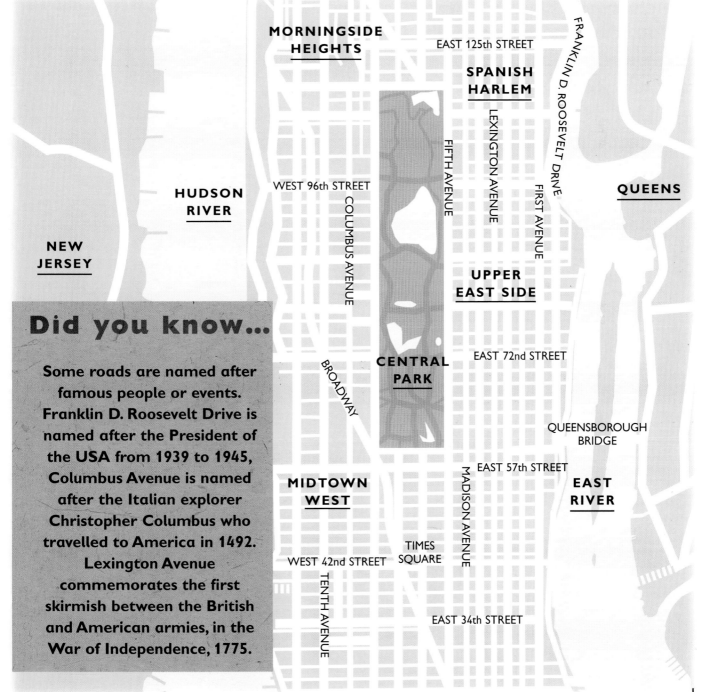

Did you know...

Some roads are named after famous people or events. Franklin D. Roosevelt Drive is named after the President of the USA from 1939 to 1945, Columbus Avenue is named after the Italian explorer Christopher Columbus who travelled to America in 1492. Lexington Avenue commemorates the first skirmish between the British and American armies, in the War of Independence, 1775.

The road of life

Some writers say that the journey we all make from birth, through life, to death is like a journey along a road. When we have to choose what we do, it can be like standing at a crossroads and deciding which road to take.

This kind of comparison is called a metaphor. In the poem, what do you think the writer is saying about the choices he has made? Is he happy with his choice?

The Road Not Taken

Two roads diverged in a yellow wood,
And sorry I could not travel both
And be one traveler, long I stood
And looked down one as far as I could
To where it bent in the undergrowth;

Then took the other, as just as fair,
And having perhaps the better claim,
Because it was grassy and wanted wear;
Though as for that, the passing there
Had worn them really about the same.

And both that morning equally lay
In leaves no step had trodden black.
Oh, I kept the first for another day!
Yet knowing how way leads on to way,
I doubted if I should ever come back.

I shall be telling this with a sigh
Somewhere ages and ages hence:
Two roads diverged in a wood, and I –
I took the one less traveled by,
And that has made all the difference.

ROBERT FROST

The Banks of Loch Lomond

In this famous song, the singer is going to be hanged and never see his native Scotland or his true love again. He calls dying "taking the low road" and says it means he will reach his beloved land before those making an ordinary journey by "the high road".

Try This!

How many stories and poems can you think of that have an important journey in them? Can you write a story or poem about a journey you have made?

By yon bonnie banks and by
  yon bonnie braes [slopes],
Where the sun shines bright on
  Loch Lomond,
Where me and my true love
  were ever wont to gae [go]
On the bonnie, bonnie banks of
  Loch Lomond.

Oh, ye'll take the high road,
  and I'll take the low road,
And I'll be in Scotland afore ye,
But me and my true love will
  never meet again,
On the bonnie, bonnie banks
  of Loch Lomond.

◄ *Today, a modern road runs alongside Loch Lomond and travellers can speed past its "bonnie banks".*

◄ *The original version of this traditional Scottish tune is quite difficult to play on the recorder. Here is a simplified version of the first four lines of the chorus for you to try.*

mf

23

Road robbers

In the past, people on the move were often an easy target for thieves. Before cheques and credit cards, travellers had to carry their money with them. Far from home, on a lonely road, they dreaded encountering an armed stranger who would demand all their valuables and leave them with no money and no means of getting home.

Number work

It is said that highwayman Dick Turpin once rode his horse Black Bess 300 km in 15 hours to give himself an alibi for a murder.

1. If Dick Turpin really made this journey, how fast did he ride in km per hour?

2. If a person set off at the same time as the highwayman, travelling on foot at 6 km per hour, how long would the journey take him?

3. How long would it take a robber today, driving a car at 120 km per hour, to make the same journey?

Highwaymen

Road robbers in the eighteenth century were known as highwaymen. They would lie in wait for travellers in order to rob them. Their cry of "Your money or your life!" struck fear into the heart of many a traveller.

Highwaymen chose lonely roads, knowing that they could ride more quickly than a coach and horses could travel. Even so, they were often caught. Dick Turpin, one of Britain's most notorious highwaymen, was hanged in the city of York in 1739.

THE TALE OF BLACK BART

Robbing stagecoaches is as much part of American Wild West folklore as sheriffs and shoot-outs, but many tales are based on true-life events. One famous robber was Charles E. Boles, or 'Black Bart'.

Black Bart was born in England in 1829, but grew up in New York State after his parents emigrated in 1831. The idea of following in his father's footsteps as a country farmer did not appeal to young Charles. So, in 1849, he left home to join the California Gold Rush. He did well enough to stay on as miner for the next ten years. He fought in the Civil War for five years on the Union side, but mining seemed tame after the adventurous life of a soldier. Charles stuck it out until 1875, when something snapped. No one knows for sure what happened, but he robbed his first stagecoach in July that year.

Witnesses told of a polite man with a shotgun and covered from head to foot in old flour sacks. Strangest of all was his habit of leaving a poem at the scene. He became known as 'Black Bart' after a character in a story, but passengers had nothing to fear. He never stole their valuables, only money from the stagecoach strong boxes. Over thirty hold-ups were blamed on Black Bart, and a price of $800 was put on his head. His downfall was a handkerchief dropped at the scene of a robbery. Detectives traced a laundry mark on it to San Francisco, and the owner was identified as respectable mining engineer Charles Boles.

After serving four years in San Quentin jail, Black Bart never robbed another stagecoach. He walked out of a San Francisco lodging house in February 1888, leaving all his belongings behind, and was never seen again.

Roads all around us

Who uses the roads around your school and home? Watch from a convenient window for fifteen minutes at three different times during the day. Mark a chart like the one below with the road-users you see pass.

It may be easier to work in pairs, especially if the road is busy. One of you can mark the chart while the other calls out what is passing. Your marks will be easier to add up at the end if you mark them in fives like this: 卌.

The road through Ashland, New Hampshire, USA, looks quiet at midday, but traffic will build up at peak times.

Users of Church street	10am	1pm	4pm
Pedestrians	卌 IIII	III	卌 II
Cars	卌	IIII	卌 II
Lorries	卌 III	II	IIII
Farm vehicles	I	I	O
Animals	I	IIII	O
Bicycles	III	O	II
Motorbikes	II	卌	II
Heavy machinery	I	I	I

What do you find? If there are traffic jams, make a note of those, too. Does the time of day make a difference? Compare your results with those of your friends who looked at different roads.

You could make a graph like the ones below to show who uses the roads surveyed. What do you think could be done to improve the flow of traffic on the roads?

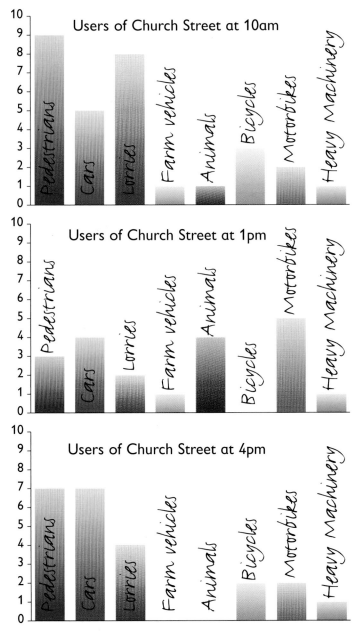

Users of Church Street at 10am

Users of Church Street at 1pm

Users of Church Street at 4pm

← At very busy times of the day, traffic may move very, very slowly. Which of the vehicles here do you think are causing the biggest problem?

Number work

Do your own survey of your class to find out how children come to school. By car? On foot? By bus? You could also ask children to find out how their parents went to school. Have things changed in the last 20 years?
Ask your grandparents, too! What happened 40 or 50 years ago, when they were children?

What's more...

Fewer roads, please!

Some people think we already have enough roads. They say that roads are using up more and more of the countryside. We should be trying to reduce the amount of traffic, not giving it more space! Sometimes, people try to stop new roads being built by refusing to move from the land to be used. What do you think about such protests?

➡ *Huge highways, such as this one being built in Mexico City, eat up vast areas of countryside.*

⬆ *Protesters go to great lengths, such as sleeping in hammocks in trees, to try to stop them being cut down to make way for new roads.*

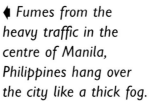

◀ *Fumes from the heavy traffic in the centre of Manila, Philippines hang over the city like a thick fog.*

◀ *A fast road speeds past McIndoe Falls, Vermont, USA. Without it, the centre of the town would be clogged with traffic.*

More roads, please!

Roads get busier all the time. What was once a quiet lane through a village may now be a noisy main road. People living nearby may ask for a bypass to be built, so that the traffic goes around the village instead of through it. Do you think this is a good idea?

Did you know...

There are roads at sea! You may have heard of shipping lanes, which are areas through which it is safe for ships to pass. Maps of the sea are also sometimes marked with "roads", avoiding sandbanks and shallow water.

Glossary

aggregate: broken rocks and stones beaten down or mixed into concrete to make a firm base for a road.

bitumen: a sticky black or brown tar-like substance made from oil and used to give a waterproof surface to roads.

brae: a steep bank

camber: a sloping surface on a road that allows water to drain away.

civil war: a war between two groups of people from the same country.

crosswind: a strong wind blowing across a road that can be dangerous for high-sided vehicles.

font: the letters of the alphabet designed with a particular shape. A computer can print out text in lots of different fonts.

friction: the force created when two things rub against each other. Friction slows down movement and gives off heat.

Gold Rush: the movement of great numbers of people towards an area where gold has been discovered. In 1849, thousands of people rushed to California when gold was discovered there.

Industrial Revolution: a period from the eighteenth to the early nineteenth century when machines and methods of manufacturing developed very quickly.

Number work answers

p5 Reading the road. 1) Because that is the main city. 2) No. There is a ring road around the city so traffic can avoid the centre. 3) There are towns on the coast that may be busy ports or have good beaches that attract tourists.

p8 Number work. 1) 5.5 days. 2) 14 days (two weeks). 3) 42 days (six weeks).

p13 Spot the difference. 1) All the roads are straight and cross each other at right angles. 2(a) The open market place was built probably first, because this is where merchants and farmers would meet to buy and sell goods. 2(b) The roads in the village were built as and when more houses were needed when the population grew. Therefore, they were not planned at one time like the roads in the city. 3) No. Traffic can go faster on straight roads, but pedestrians are safer where traffic has to travel more slowly.

pp14–15 (a) crossroads ahead. (b) series of bends. (c) Left turn ahead; 60 miles per hours speed limit. (d) No right turn. (e) Bicycles only. (f) Clearway – no stopping. (g) Harbour.

p17 Map reading. 1) 2.1 km. 2) 4.5 km. 3(a) A windmill (b) 6.3km. 4) 1 hour 45 minutes (10.5 km at 60 km per hour).

p18 Number work. 25m.

p21 Number work. 1) 8. 2) 24.

p24. Number work. 1) 20 km per hour. 2) 50 hours (two days and two hours). 3) 2.5 hours.

Glossary

juggernaut: a large and heavy truck.

junction: the place where two or more roads meet, such as a crossroads.

landmarks: buildings, hills, bridges and other features that stand out in the landscape and help travellers to find their way.

mass-produced: items made in quantity in factories so that they are exactly the same and can be made very quickly.

merchant: someone who buys and sells things for a living.

Middle Ages: a period in history from around AD 1000 to AD 1450.

monument: a building or other structure that is put up in memory of a person or an event.

mortar: a mixture of lime or cement, sand and water used to join bricks and stones together.

network: the pattern in which roads or lines meet and join.

parallel: lines or structures that are always the same distance apart. Parallel lines never meet.

pilgrimage: a journey taken for religious reasons, such as to visit the shrine of a holy person, or to mark a special event.

planners: people who work out how and where roads and buildings are to be built.

reaction time: the time that passes between a driver seeing a problem and reacting to it.

right angle: an angle of exactly 90°.

Roman Empire: a huge area of Europe and parts of Africa and Asia controlled by the Romans. It was at its largest around AD 100.

shrine: a place where a saint or other holy person is remembered, perhaps because his or her body is buried there.

Silk Road: a route between Europe and China used from around 300 BC. Traders carried silk, spices and many other goods along it.

survey: an overall view of a subject or place, usually obtained by taking measurements.

tarmacadam: a mixture of tar and stones used to surface a road.

trade: buying and selling goods.

Index

accidents 11, 18
adventure 7
aggregate 11, 29

Banks of Loch Lomond, The 23
Bart, Black 25
bicycles 4, 7, 26
bitumen 10, 29
buses 4, 7, 27
bypass 29

camber 10, 11, 29
carriages 10
cars 4, 11, 26, 27
cement 10
chariots 6
cities 4, 5, 13
concrete 8, 11
countryside 4, 11, 12, 28
crash barriers 11
crossroads 22
cyclists 7, 18

danger 18
drivers 14, 18

Flecker, James Elroy 7
Freeway, San Diego 11

friction 12
four-wheel drive 7
Ford, Model T 7
Frost, Robert 22

highway 28
Highway, Pan American 11
highwaymen 24
horse-drawn vehicles 6, 10

Industrial Revolution 10, 29

juggernauts 11, 29

landscape 11, 12
lorries 11, 26

main road 17
maps 16
motorists 18, 19
motorways 17
mountains 12

network 28, 31

pedestrians 26
penny farthing 7
pilgrimages 9, 31

road of life 22–23
Road to Samarkand, The 7
road names 21
Road Not Taken, The 22
roads, Roman 8
roadbuilding 10, 11, 12, 13
road planning 13
robbers 24–25
routes 5

safety 18
Silk Road 6, 31
signs, road 14–15
slip road 11
speed 12, 18
stagecoach 6, 25
steel bars 11
stone-age roller 6

tarmacadam 10, 11, 31
towns 4, 13, 29
tracks 4, 9
traffic 4, 8, 11, 18, 26, 27, 28, 29
trails 4
transport
travellers 7, 24

trucks 4
tunnels 12
Turpin, Dick 24

villages 13, 29

wagon 6, 10

Yellow Brick Road 7